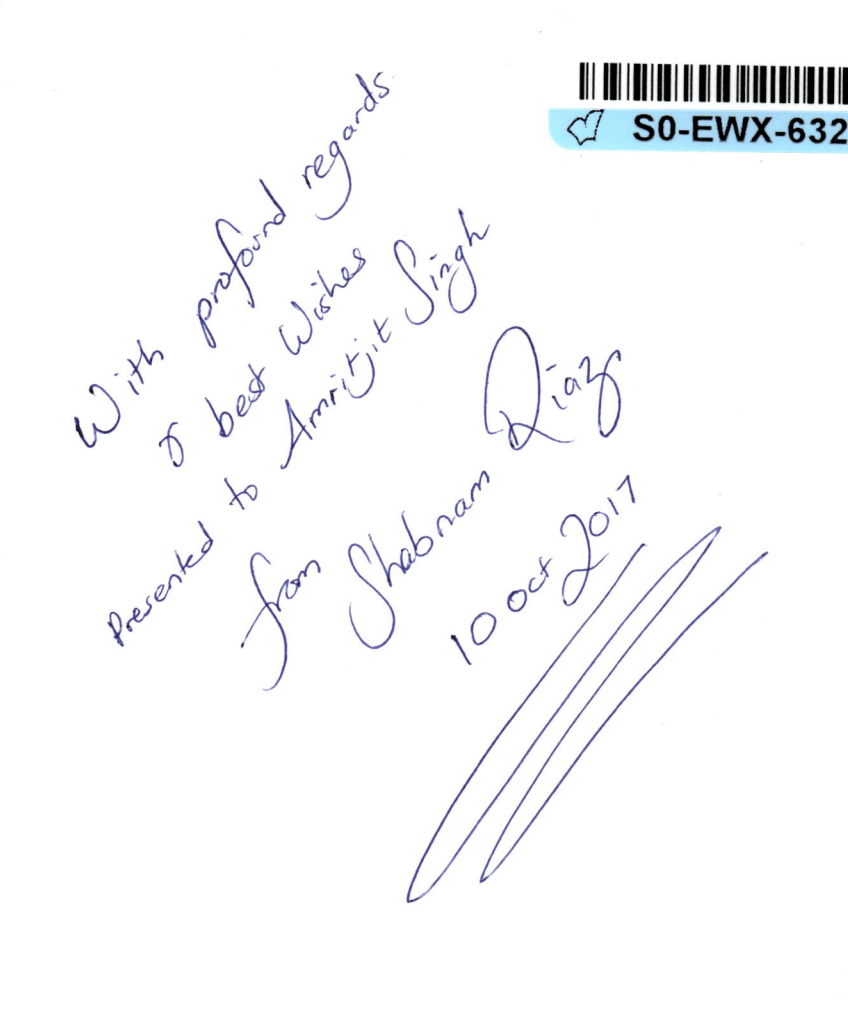

With profound regards
& best wishes
Presented to Amritjit Singh
from Shabnam Riaz
10 Oct 2017

The Whispering Wind

by
Shabnam Nasir

All Rights Reserved

NBF 1st Print 2006	:	1000 Copies
Code No	:	GNE-284
Printed by	:	Marshal Printing Press Rawalpindi.
ISBN	:	969-37-0218-2

**National Book Foundation
Islamabad**

THE PRESIDENT
Islamic Republic of Pakistan

Foreword
By
General Pervez Musharraf
President of the Islamic Republic of Pakistan

I was delighted to go through this collection of poetry by Shabnam Nasir. The work is moving, touches the soul and is a manifestation of her high intellect. I am also deeply impressed by the manner in which she has very eloquently woven into simple and touching verse, the various intricacies of life, nature and human relationships.

I am sure her poetic work will make absorbing reading for people of all ages. My favourite poem is titled "To My Mother", which is a tribute to the most wonderful of all relationships – between a mother and child.

I wish Shabnam all the success in her further intellectual pursuits.

General
(Pervez Musharraf)
17 May, 2005

To my family;

As it has been their love, support and faith that has always given me strength.

About The Author

Shabnam Nasir was born and raised in London. She wrote her first poem at the age of seven which was published in a popular girl's magazine in Britain. After coming to settle in Pakistan with her parents, the many social, cultural and political issues inspired her to write as a freelance writer for various English newspapers. Her main contributions include writing regularly for Pakistan's most widely circulated English newspaper, 'The Daily Dawn,' for The Review, Books and Authors and the Education page.

Working in the media led her to pursue a career in television where she is a news anchor for the national television network; PTV.

The Whispering Wind is her first collection of poetry to be published and is inspired by the current events of today's world; the relationships that make up life; and the fundamentals of human nature that shape destiny and eventually contribute in making ones history.

Her poetry is an integral part of her life and every poem is shaped according to the mood that dictates them. The themes of her verse are drawn from the state of humanity, philosophical explorations, nature's diversities and the substance of relations merged into poetic verse. Like a typical poet, her feeling dictates her writing which contain ingredients of mischief, humour and sentimentality-with the essential sprinkling of philosophy for the reader to feast on.

She resides in Islamabad with her husband who is a doctor working for The National Institute of Health and her three daughters, Ayesha, Mariam and Myra.

INTRODUCTION

It was a humid day in late July and my children's summer vacations were nearly at an end, but unfortunately, so was my patience. My three daughters mean the world to me, but their endless reserves of abundant energy often leaves me exhausted. Combining this situation with a demanding television career and writing assignments to be completed before impending deadlines, meant I was basically mentally and physically stretched.

On one particular day when all three of my kids were running riot at home, and I was contemplating whether I had enough stamina to chase them round the house, I decided to instead pen a humorous account (an exaggerated version of course) in poetic verse. This decision resulted in my writing one of my favourite poems *'to my sister'* which proved to me that laughter really is the best medicine. After my children had overcome the initial indignation and offense at what they perceived as an unfair portrayal, the ball was set rolling for me to start writing down whatever suited my mood on a particular day.

Although I had been writing poems throughout my life I never thought of compiling them. It was only until one day, when my father told me that he enjoyed reading them and suggested that I should collect my work to form a book, that I thought of gathering my poems together.

Once I had seriously started writing poetry and started giving quite some time in somber reflections, my family were the victims of my effort and regardless of time I would impose on them 'my latest work.' It got so bad that they started dreading the vision of me with a folder in my hands and would busy themselves immediately in furious activity! However , no one can outmaneuver a poet is what I say, and like it or not they had to give in sooner or later- an incentive for my work *'never become a poet.'*

I have to say that writing is a part of me that has become an essential ingredient of my life. Whether it is writing articles on the many social and economic problems that need to be solved or recording verse on a sudden idea that grips a thought- I have always turned to a pen and paper as a most trusted friend and my needed medium of expression. A world without words would definitely be like spring without flowers, and it is these scented blossoms that lift spirits and lighten the soul in the journey we take through unknown paths.

I believe that poetry is a gift of memories, reflections and quiet ponderings of the mind and spirit that may fill many an empty heart with tenderness and inspiration.

Shabnam Nasir
14 September 2005

ACKNOWLEDGMENTS

There are many people who I am extremely grateful to who encouraged and supported me in the materialization of this work. When I presented a manuscript of my poems to the President, General Pervez Musharraf, I did not really think he would actually get the time to read them. (You know being consumed with other matters like foreign policy; terrorism; confidence building measures with India e.t.c.) so when he sent me the Foreword on my poetry and said he really enjoyed reading my work, I felt that I had finally reached some stature in the field of literature! Needless to say, my family's attitude also changed and they actually started asking to see my work. I am extremely grateful to General Pervez for taking out his valuable time to study my work and writing a foreword that gives me immense pleasure every time I read it.

I am also deeply grateful to the President's mother, Mrs. Zareen Musharraf, who also took great interest in reading all my poems and regularly follows all the various articles I write. She has always been most encouraging throughout the various aspects of my career, especially in my anchoring the news on PTV, and was always very insistent that I publish my work. I deeply appreciate her generous praise and high esteem that she has always regarded me in. I can easily say that I have learnt a lot from her very gracious and lovely personality.

I am also very grateful to Mr. Iftikhar Arif, Chairman Pakistan Academy of Letters, who took out his valuable time to study my work and offer me the right guidance and support in the development of my book. I deeply appreciate the encouragement and direction he showed me in my passion for writing poetry.

I also thank Mr. Amjad Islam Amjad who was very kind to go through my work and offer his words of appreciation.

Finally, I would also like to offer my many thanks and gratitude to my uncle, Mr. Jameel Siddiqui who provided me with invaluable guidance and support in the many hurdles that lie between writing and publishing- I am very grateful to him for keeping the momentum going when the pace slowed down.

CONTENTS

To my mother	1
Whispering wind	2
Make your mark	3
She was a stranger to me	4
The courageous ones	7
Grammar rules	9
Tomorrow is our challenge	10
Nature's balm	13
History is written	14
To sow your dream	15
My prayers	17
Land, Sea, Air	18
Picking up the pieces	20
Maybe	22
To my sister	23
My treasures	24
The smallest things	26
An empty vase	27
The essence of life	29
Timeless tree	30
The dishonoured one	32
The strongest power	34
The sea of life	36
She spoke those words	37

A loving hand	39
I saw you	40
The memory box	42
Crossing over	44
The searching soul	46
Say a thousand words	48
The land of daisies	49
Wondrous things	50
Your faithful companion	51
The fairy in a buttercup	53
Waiting	55
What hunger is	58
To live a whole life	61
History is witness	64
Tears are not a sign of weakness	66
My modest bouquet	67
We need to find	69
Never become a poet	71
Just a little care	73
Those vicious of tongue	74
Spring	75
A land of beauty	76
Enjoying Basant	77
True love	78
Silent tears	79
Climb any mountain	80

TO MY MOTHER

I can never repay all that you have done,
Whenever I called, I knew you would come.
Forever friend -A wiper of tears;
Your prized words of wisdom erasing my fears.
Loving voice, to soothe all pain
Helping to lift my spirits again.
Always ready, to carry my load
When walking along life's rugged road.
Your prayers for me are the strongest wall
Between all evils, big or small.

The garden you nurtured has long reached full bloom,
The flowers that blossomed now spread their perfume.
All that we achieve is because of your love,
There's no doubt about it- You're a gift from above.
You have always been there -you have always been true.
I just wish I may be
As great a mother as you.

****

WHISPERING WIND

Oh wondrous, mystic,
Whispering wind,
What secrets lie within the air?
Of sounds once known
To lovers' songs,
Who promised everlasting care.

What hidden myths
Were swept ahead
To make their way through eras gone.
The wars they lost;
The hearts they won;
The cries of time still float along.

But you have known
Each hill and plain,
And been to every darkest cave.
Then graced the oceans
With your touch,
To shape the mood of every wave.

So take these words
Along with you,
To sweep the earth's each fold and crease.
Caress all ears
With prayers of love,
Become the breeze that preaches peace.
****

MAKE YOUR MARK

Walk not on crumbling sand
For when you look back to see
If your footprints are still there,
They will have been washed away
By the morning tide.
For even though the soft surface
Is so tempting,
It cannot hold its own substance
Let alone your dreams.

Better to choose
The rough terrain,
Seemingly hostile and hard beneath your feet,
But when you leave your mark
Those imprints will be timeless,
For all to see.

****

SHE WAS A STRANGER TO ME

She was a stranger to me
Who I did not know,
So frail and so thin,
But her eyes held a glow,
That lit her spirit
As if from within,
Giving her strength
To those shoulders so slim.

I had recently seen her,
Each day standing there,
Her eyes looking at me,
Continuing to stare.
Her gaze held a story
For those who wanted to see;
A whisper for help,
A silent plea.

'Tomorrow' I thought,
I'll give her warm clothes and my shawl,
To keep her from shivering
While standing there, by that wall.
But 'tomorrow' became
An excuse each day,
As I kept on forgetting
Her things on my way.

Then one night there came
A freezing cold storm,
Next day, I saw her children,
Alone and forlorn.
In the same place they stood
As their mother had, each day
Now their eyes swum with tears
-No one to wipe them away.

I hurried over to them,
Heavy bag in my hand,
Knowing not what to say-
I had nothing planned.
'Please take these things,
The weather's so cold,
Give this shawl to your mother
She seems so frail and so old.

Their eyes full of questions,
But they hurriedly dressed
In all that I gave them,
'Till the shawl was left.
The eldest then handed
The bag back to me,
Shaking her head
So silently.

'We do not have a mother'
Said she, 'not at all,
She died years ago,
Right here, by this wall.'
And with that they left
-But their eyes had a glow

And she was a stranger to me
Who I did not know.

****

THE COURAGEOUS ONES

Just because his mouth was dry
And his legs were trembling
It did not mean he had no courage.
For it took a real man to stand where he was.

Looking straight ahead
Unwavering glance never leaving
The eyes of his opponent.
Steady gaze met and locked-
Each trying to out stare the other,
But both were built of a steady resolve
That had overcome many battles before.

They stood rooted,
Each waiting for the other to surrender
His position.
But as the minutes flew by
Time knew no friend.
And then came the call-
The siren that rang
Alerted all senses,
And adrenaline rushed into every vein.
They knew this was their last chance
To get what they had desired;
That waiting now reaching its climax.

And as those glass doors opened

The mad rush grew into a frenzy
As the shoppers went wild
On the last winter sale!

****

GRAMMAR RULES

Have you ever stopped to wonder why
It makes no difference how you try
To understand the different rules
When learning English grammar at school.

Just when you think you've got it right
And your future's looking bright
There's the page of indirect speech
That your teacher has to teach.

And when you've mastered adverb clauses
The use of commas and their pauses,
The same word 'read' can also be said
To change its sound, and be spoken as 'red'.

Where antonyms and synonyms
Appear to have a grip on things
Silent letters give your brain a twist
When spelling words like psychiatrist.

Homophones may sound the same
If you get confused, you're knot to blame.
For, if you reed sum books they'll tell
There knot sow alike, when you spell.

You have got to be careful in all that you say
There's a right place in saying 'I can' or 'I may'.
Whether we can, or whether we might
We may just keep on trying to get it all right!
****

TOMORROW IS OUR CHALLENGE

Yesterday is just a memory.

Yesterday, all was right with the world.
When playful children laughed and teased
their way to school, after being kissed goodbye
by loving parents who had no idea that they would
never see them again.

Today is an agonizing torment.

A terror that struck deep in every heart,
when the earth so angrily shook its being -as
if to say it no longer wanted mankind on its
substance.
Like the mighty lion who tosses his mane, growling
and emitting a fierce roar -
striking terror in every heart.

It took just a few minutes to wipe
away history from the face of the map-
a whole generation lost to bricks and dust.
While the living screamed agonized sobs
of suffering, the dying lay waiting on
borrowed breaths-hoping for a faded sound
of someone calling out- or was it just
the sounds of the dead moaning
against the blackest of nights?

But in the darkest depths, can be found a
ray of light.
As He who sends down calamities
also sends His angels from
above to work miracles. Walking the earth
and carrying blessings on wings that
sweep away the doom of death. And the
cheers and sobs of joy pierce the air as
out of the thousands dead, a survivor
is pulled out alive.

Today we found hope.

As this nation has done us proud.
When calls were answered in the blink of an eye
and young and old; rich and poor knew no divide-
working as one to reach a common desire.
For there is no motivation as strong
or no power so moving as the resolve
of a volunteer.

Today humanity called out loud.

And the world answered back.
For every tear that has been shed
we must bring so many smiles.
For every fallen village that has been lost
we must build a thriving town.
Yes, it will take time, many years if
needed.

But we will prevail;
We will succeed;
As once the spirit is there- many paths are to be found.

Tomorrow is our challenge, our destiny.

For our country needs us now
more than ever in the past. And our hearts all beat as one
as we are ready to rise
as a nation born again. Never forgetting the test
put before us, and our steady resolve
that will be needed in times to come.

So let's say a silent prayer. A commitment that we will always remember. A determination that
while always being true
to others we will also be true to ourselves.
So spread the message of humanity, as there will always be the haunting unknown, between Yesterday and Today.

****

NATURE'S BALM

A
Liquid drop.

Sometimes as furious
As a lava flow,
Or often cooling-
Soothing away pain.
Rushing forth,
As the swollen dam
That bursts its banks
After a heavy storm.
Or spilling slowly,
Over the rim of the vessel
That can hold no more.

Burning its path downwards
On glistening skin,
It is nature's balm
For when the
Heart overflows.

****

HISTORY IS WRITTEN

History is written
For everyone to see,
You are with us or without us;
Oppression reigns supreme.

History is repeated
Power is the song,
All tunes which sound unpleasant
Will sing to whistling bombs.

History is being written
The lessons are the same,
Terrorism? Imperialism?
Just whom should we blame?

****

TO SOW YOUR DREAM

Sow your dream-
Let its sleepy seeds lie in rich, promising soil,
give it patience, love
And hope- allow it considerable
Days of toil.

Watch it grow-

Look carefully for that
Tiny shoot of brilliant, vibrant, peep of
Green,
It's made its way through
Stones and mud until it finally
Can be seen.

Protect it well-

When the earth does crack,
Then water it well, when floods
Do threat then build a wall.
Show it strength and nurture well,
Then watch it sprout
And shoot up tall.

Have no fears-

When aimless hailstones hurtle down
And heavy rains give no relief,
Stand your ground and ease your mind
With silent prayers and strong belief.

Make it come true-

When that unassuming bud unwraps to
Face up to the sun,
pluck it , press it to
Heart's folds; to be now fulfilled-
The time has come.

****

MY PRAYERS

Morning breaks,
Swallows fly,
Filling up the new dawn sky.
May you seek
Then find your dream,
And float your way through nature's stream.
Always finding waters calm,
Wrapped around you like a balm.
When night falls
And stars do shine;
Remember all these prayers of mine

****

LAND, SEA AND AIR

If sorrows were not born
The value of joy would cease,
For every ravaged nation torn ,
Burns harder the will for peace.

Do sparkle diamond flecks
In blackest nights so deep
As the sun does humbly bow
So creatures great and small may sleep.

While dawn and dusk do play
To their tunes of hide and seek
Eroding landscapes groan
As once mighty shapes turn weak.

And one soul will breathe his last
So another screams for air
While placed in his mother's arms
Who'll vow eternal care.

For Land, Sea and Air
Are being borrowed – Nothing's new,
To share essentials all
Is what we came to do.

And while death's angel stalks
Every minute, every day,
Our deeds are written firm,
In all we do; in all we say.

****

PICKING UP THE PIECES

I spent a long time
picking up the pieces of
the China vase that slipped
out of my hands
without warning.

I thought I had it clenched
firmly in my grasp but
it took me by surprise
when it shattered on the
floor below-
rudely jolting me
out of my thoughts.

I looked down- aghast.
This had been a piece
passed through generations.
But then I instantly comforted
myself when I remembered
it had known accidents before.

I then did what others prior to
me had.
Lovingly; painstakingly,
joining jagged edges together
concealing cracks as best
as could.
However now, the lazy lines were

more evident on the smooth, ceramic
surface.
but, to me, it would make no
difference. As the wrinkled
face of an old woman can still
command the appreciation of
a devoted admirer's loving glance.

And through the
wear and tear of time,
I know my precious vase can fall
again, regardless of how
I protect it from harm.
So I made an inner
resolve.
That after the initial pain
I will just spend an even
longer time,
if needed,
in picking up the pieces again.

****

MAYBE

Watching the sunrise, another day is born
New hopes soar, she whispers fresh prayers again,
As their heavy hearts beat with the sound of his name.
Maybe, he will come home today.

Valiant soldier, distant battles await,
You leave behind your laughter, your whispers in the wind,
Your possessions lie untouched, the same is everything.
Maybe your smile will fill the house today.

She knelt to pick her son, their cheeks held shimmering streams,
While the morning breeze swept by and carried their tears
To a nearby hill, caressing his gentle face
Where he lay silent;
Embracing the ground in eternal peace.

****

TO MY SISTER

I wanted to see you yesterday,
But I slipped on some paint in my way,
Instead, I'll see the doctor today.
But still, I love my kids!

Remember the chair we used to play in?
Passing along generations within,
Well, It crashed to the floor with an awful din.
But still, I love my kids!

I invited my boss for dinner today,
Let's hope everything goes my way,
Maybe I should just sit and pray.
But still, I love my kids!

I never could tell why you stopped coming round,
Was it because your ring was never found?
Or that time when your shed burned down to the ground?
But still, I love my kids!

The angels are sleeping, but it took a long while
To retrieve the dog safely, from under the pile
Of broken bricks-but he still managed to smile
-Because everyone loves my kids!

MY TREASURES

You both were always there,
Through those nights black and deep,
When we all stayed awake,
Just because I could not sleep.

Every toothache we shared,
All those tummy aches you soothed,
Your spirit lifting words
To mend anything I bruised.

And those walks in the park
-Little legs could hardly stand,
But I stumbled all the way
As you held my tiny hands.

Those endless playground fights,
That you always tried to fix,
And I told you, "no,
I can handle this, I'm six!"

When I found myself in tears,
In your lap and soothing arms,
I knew I had no fears
And that I would be safe from harm.

Then the years tumbled by,
To find babies of my own,
As I struggled with their care,
I thought more and more of home.

And now I will take your hands,
To give you all my strength,
So we can walk in the park,
With your slowly taken steps.

And I promise to be there
To stay awake when you can't sleep,
While I deeply will thank God
For the treasures I may keep.

****

THE SMALLEST THINGS

From the weakest of voices
Can rise the strongest cry
Giving voice to a nation that turns its tide.

It's the tiniest of creatures
Can move the heaviest of loads
Working together as a purposeful team.

While the smallest of acts
May be the most oft' remembered
-So don't think of power as a measure of size.

****

AN EMPTY VASE

An empty vase
awaits its
occupants
while sitting idle;
unassuming.

Crystalline glints
are momentary
eye catchers
but can't boast
of holding
a gaze.
Morning lights
transform to
evening chandeliers
reflecting dancing
prisms-
but still, nothing
fills the void.

But for now, it
may be content
to wait out its
loneliness, as its
promised visitors
have been
destined instead
to adorn the newly
turned soil of
a quiet grave.

****

THE ESSENCE OF LIFE

Coming forth into the world
Claiming immortality,
We rush about the earth;
Triumphant, defeated, victorious, oppressed.
Horrific images of war-ravaged nations
Touch our hearts for a while,
'Till we forget.

Savouring moments of self-centered joy,
Entwining destinies will bring us together again.
Traveling along life's green mile,
What is it we are seeking?

When our bones decay and mingle with the earth
Will we really know the essence of life.

****

TIMELESS TREE

The dry winding road
Sweeps high on the hill
Touching the fort
Where the walls are so still,
And the dusty old bricks
Tell a story so true
But to look at it now,
You'd be somewhat confused.

That where ever you walk
On the ground underfoot
There were royals and nobles
Who so proudly all stood.
Then how did the era
So great and so grand
Succumb to humility
And give up this land?

For the towering walls
Now guard tombs of the brave
And stand silent witness
To sacrifices made.
And the ghosts wander far
From a hundred summers past
The only life that sustained
Was this tree that has last.
Through the winters and fall
From invaders and raids

This is the place
Where history was made.

But in the dead of the night
When the quiet is high
You can hear branches groaning
And the leaves that do sigh.
As the burden of time
Has weighed lush foliage down
As time stops for none
Neither beggar nor crown.

****

THE DISHONOURED ONE

She was created after you
-not as an afterthought,
But because you needed companionship,
To share moments and
Give each other strength.

You may have walked on the moon
And changed history,
But she was given a miracle
No man could ever boast of-
The marvel of giving life
As ordained by the creator.
It was she who gave you those sons
Who went to war,
And then nursed back the wounded
From the wars you started.

She gave you might
In more ways then one
And stood side by side, working
In fields waiting to be harvested
And in making houses into homes.

So then why in this world
Did you abuse her and strip her of all honour;
Robbing her pride
And made being feminine, a curse for her to bear.
But when all will stand equal
In front of the Lord
-when that day will come-
She will look into your eyes
And ask,
Tell me, who is the dishonoured one now?

****

THE STRONGEST POWER

When the heart is heavy
From life's load, and weary is
The soul within, darkest seem the
Coming days, as grieving is so genuine.

How can you tell all
Those who say, 'I understand, just
How you feel.' That actually they
Have no grasp, of the intense and searing pain you feel.

You want to go
And find a space, a silent
Corner or retreat, to make some sense
Of fates' cruel blows and try to ease that heavy beat.

But while you look
Inside yourself, you'll be amazed
At what you'll find. An inner force
That slowly blooms, a peaceful strength
Will fill your mind.

And when the bleakness starts to
Change, by toiling past
The winter days, the new spring sun will
Gently shine and quietly clear up all the haze.

So trust in God and do
Not loose, the strongest power
That is faith, as he will guide you
Knowingly, so that your life
Falls into place.

****

THE SEA OF LIFE

The sea of life beckons to me
Glistening and serene,
Sparkling lights fly, at tangents to the waves,
Glittering jewels float in peaceful slumber-
A dreamers haven, is here for all.

Distant echoes moan, as silhouettes of dark clouds appear,
The horizon takes an ominous stare
At the expanse of Majesty beneath
A vengeful soldiers' wrath, is here for all.

Return the clearing skies, eruptions subside,
The song is now of a friendlier tune,
Tranquility returns, nature's rivals are at rest
But I do not trust, what is here for all.

****

SHE SPOKE THOSE WORDS

She spoke those words
That glided along the length of the room
-So distant yet so far.
That whisper;
Echoed in his ears
To spin a web of
Eternal desire,
Forming silken heart strings
That tugged at his soul-
For now he was alone.

But as the shadow breezed past
He again felt her cool touch
Sliding smoothly,
Just for a moment
Along his face.

No denying the presence;
Though fleeting,
He was sure.
For that scent of jasmine that hung
Heavily in the night,
Came not from
Velvet petals,
But had been born from those lips
That uttered his name.

As he drew fresh tears
That slowly slithered
Meandering along
Parched skin,
His body sank
Crumbling to the ground,
And he answered
In one breath-
'I am here'.

****

A LOVING HAND

A single prayer, a soothing word,
A reassuring gaze,
May sometimes be the strongest step
In walking through life's maze.

To find your way through ups and downs
Amongst a tear or laugh,
We need to find a loving hand
To reach our chosen path.

So don't forget the rules of life
When playing out the game,
That what you give is what you get
-For all, it works the same.

****

I SAW YOU
(A tribute to the Tsunami victims)

I saw you.

Right in front of me,
Screaming, crying,
Pleading for help.
I wanted to reach out
And help you,
As the ocean spent its wrath
Ravaging all in its path,
But land and sea had become one.

I saw you.

Gasping for breath,
Clinging to that tree
With your last ounces of strength,
Praying that a miracle would happen.
But hell had arrived on earth
As the forces of nature combined,
To show man how insignificant he is
Against the powers of the divine.

I saw you.

Just before you were swept away,
And that terror stricken face told me
You had seen the angel of death.
Then you were sucked afar,
To become a tiny dot-
Lost into oblivion.

I stood still.

Silent witness to death and destruction
Frozen in shock-
I had done nothing.
Not even lifted a finger to help
Or moved a muscle.
I was immobilised by
Those horrific scenes.
Wishing it had not happened;
Wishing I had not seen.
But after I had switched off my television set
I could not get you out of my mind.
I closed my eyes, to see
Your face
And those haunted eyes.

****

THE MEMORY BOX

A forgotten scent drifts slowly by
That memory box is opened wide,
Senses muddled just a while,
Recollections force a smile
To creep across a furrowed frown
And lighten thoughts of one who's down.

Cascading images of time
Spilling dominoes in a line,
Transported back to early years
The salty taste of tiny tears
That welled up instantaneously,
From damaged pride or burning knees.

The only worries seemed to be
How to climb the big oak tree
Whose branches beckoned tall and proud
As if to mock and say aloud,
'seek your luck to touch the sky
Or be content to never try.'

When childhood giggles pierced the air
And everyone looked round to stare,
But teacher dear was not amused
And left no mind likewise confused
To what she thought of pranks and fools
Or those who dared to joke in school.

Those guilty faces gave away
The mightiest lie on any day
When asked who sneaked into the store
And scattered cake crumbs on the floor.

So keep the memory box ajar
And take deep breaths of near and far,
For when we next inhale in a dream
-The past's not as far as it may seem.

****

CROSSING OVER

Sweeping past myriad dimensions-
Monuments stand still, while
Time does not. Testaments to
Forgotten eras; as power has
Been lost to sand and dust.

Born to live, but living
To die, what can be more natural
Than to accept a journey's
Final destination?
Ancestors always waiting to claim those
Crossing over, a luminous glow
Shines as life itself withers
Away from lids fighting not
To close. But how to
Escape the inevitable, where succumbing
Is beginning.
And there they wait.
Arms open, hungry for the very
Embrace that tore them apart in another existence.

Run lighthearted to the radiant light. Past fears to
Longing arms and voices that will
Lead over misty plains to
Promised gardens. Finding
Destiny amongst those who were loved and
Lost. Loose yourself in the grip of those
You only met in distant dreams, that heartbreaking

Thirst now to be quenched.
Pure; revitalizing; nectar- sweet
From cascading waterfalls
Will absolve all sins in
The fountain of youth. Enter the
World again- but now
Immortal and fearless.

****

THE SEARCHING SOUL

Seek not heaven in
This land that promises
Immortality to the vain. As
Such serenity illuminates only
The Lion hearted who dare
To look beyond themselves
Content with other's joys.

Tranquil beaches spread
Before a searching soul,
Where the future and past
Merge on the shores
Of time. Majestic waves
Sweep along memories of etched
Mystic shadows
On glistening gold, then hastily,
Sneak back to the oceans
Loving call.

Déjà vu confuses,
Perplexes.
As a spirit confirms its
Earlier presence of a
Preceding era.

So between heaven and earth
There lies a great divide
Where spiritual forces collide
And disperse in a celestial canopy.
There lie the answers to
The questions of many a
Wandering heart.

This quest is where steps will
Only answer to the beckoning
Of the soul and mind.

****

SAY A THOUSAND WORDS

Why don't you say a thousand words
In a silent message sent,
That leaps past boundaries undefined
To say you are a friend.

It crosses every language known
Can shorten a distant mile,
To brighten up when feeling low
Its time you shared a smile.

****

THE LAND OF DAISIES

Why should the world go on
Living out their dreams, while watching
Murders of innocents on coloured screens?
As humanity progresses, refined
And virtuous,
and smiling graciously, when signing orders
That will ensure the slaughter of thousands-
Where daisy cutters will prettily slice
The flesh from the bone.

But in another world-
Not far from where the daisies grow-
Parents tenderly snuggle their children
In customized bedding.
While in the land of flowers,
He wraps his butchered child in a ripped cloth
To send to sleep in the depths of the earth,
Where they will soon meet,
To live out their dreams.

****

WONDROUS THINGS

Like a little grain of sand
Caught up in the desert wind,
We're tossed into each others paths
Are we controlling anything?

Like a fluttering autumn leaf
Falling to a bristling stream,
That floats to meet a river wide
How did we get to the mighty sea?

For God did make these wondrous things
To help us through life's uphill stride.
So we may thank Him everyday
For all the blessings He provides.

****

YOUR FAITHFUL COMPANION

You can hear it
At night, pulsing in your ear
Although it's been with you faithfully.
But that's when you notice the stable rhythm
That decides between now and the afterlife.
Its steady throb
Assures you that all is well,
As you leave this world
To visit the valley of dreams.

Slowly, it gathers speed
As images form, coming together
To merge into your most hidden fears.
As your chest rises and falls, to
Help the adrenaline supply
Reach those muscles poised for flight,
You face your demons in the shadows of the night.

Pumping wildly,
You race
To get the hell out of that place,
As the devil is hot on your heels.
You strive to run,
But your body is a defiant entity
And the scream you long to roar,
Dies some where in the midst of your throat.

As you toss and turn
You must be rescued from this distress,
Finally you shout for the safety of that world
Where you can run and scream
To your hearts content.
Then you are jolted by a fierce push-
Back to merciful wakefulness.

You slowly comprehend
That you are safe from the terrors of the unknown,
As your loyal friend
Releases its heavy pounding
Slowly subsiding into
The rhythmic calm that you trust so well.

And you know it will
Be your faithful companion
Until the very end.

****

THE FAIRY IN A BUTTERCUP

When walking past a rippling brook
Unseen to any near grown up,
I saw a fairy with white wings
Sitting in a buttercup.

As the water swept past rocks
That tinkled notes, which pleased the ear,
I heard her sing a tune so pure;
Nectar sweet and crystal clear.

I cautiously bent down to see
Whilst careful not to halt her song,
But she looked up to smile at me
As if she knew I'd come along.

Then she blew a prayer to me
Which fluttered lightly, full of grace
Carried by the summer breeze,
To softly brush across my face.

Instantly I felt a calm
That filled me with a deepened joy,
For I had found a special friend
Just like me- unknown and coy.

And then she spread her delicate wings
Woven from silk glistening threads,
And flew above me to the sky,
Scattering gold dust on my head.

When at home all did ask
As to how my hair did shine
With such a glow of sparkling shades
-The secret was, just hers and mine.

****

WAITING

Her lips moved
uttering a millionth request
calling for his endless slumber to cease.
But did it evoke a flutter of his lashes
or a reflex of a
hushed murmour gliding
across a sleeping face?

It had been too long.
Now waiting had become the curse
condemning her to insufferable torment.
The affliction of dull pain was
searing,
driving through her midst while
crushing the spirit in the vice
of uncertainty.

But to
give up now? When seven springs
had risen from the middle
of the bleakest winters, showing
miracles were just a moment away
waiting to be plucked from
the most unassuming blossom.

Hoping.
Praying.
But how long would faith sustain heavy
breaths that now took longer to fill
weary lungs. Fatigued, and starving
for what had always been.
Not too
distant a world ago, laughter
was thrown so casually
to the breeze. Tossed and
passed to each other through
eyes that had creased into a slant from
times that were now
far- off memories.

They told her she was playing
a dangerous game, building
dreams on vague assumptions.
But she knew what her heart was telling her;
and what others had given up on
had become her strongest compulsion.

How could she end it all at the touch
of a switch?
A simple action that would finish
his wait and hers.
They had not been there
at his bed-side
when his lips formed
that sound. A call for her to believe in him and not
let go.
They all had their own
lives to live, but
her existence was here, and
she would not let it go so easily.

She was sure
the nightmare was to end soon-
ceasing the agony of an endless wait.
And he would arise from
his endless slumber to find her with
dry eyes, yearning for
his loving gaze to quench those dried up tears.

****

WHAT HUNGER IS

Hungry eyed and heavy hearted
Looked he upon those who did sing
Of happy talk and woes departed
At a table fit to feed a king.

A lusty pain shot through his mind
And longing twisted up his chest
For when he had filled his starving soul
He could hardly reminisce.

An orphan child was he of late
Left to fend for siblings small
With empty hearts and misty eyes
They looked at him to tend to all.

The manor's door did groan ajar
And shuffled out a burly maid
Who threw a sack onto the ground
Aside the mansion's grand gold gate.

Concealed behind a stately bush
He waited for her slow return,
And then like lightening ran ahead
Focusing on his one concern.

A short, swift, sweep ensured his catch
And delighted at the heavy load
He ran out the gates with his loot
Secured on his shoulder down the road.

All at once there came a scream
That pierced the bitterly, icy air
And two strong hands grabbed
Scrawny shoulders, as his flimsy coat did
Rip and tear.

Alone, confused, pinned heavily down
He did let out a chilling scream
As looked at him five pairs of eyes
-in each gaze did hot fury gleam.

He sobbed his innocence in vain
As sturdy hands beat skinny bones
They left him there, an example to all.
For those who dared come near their home.

'Common thief' they chanted loud
Their voices echoed down the street
As bruised, he slowly raised his head
And grimly tried to get to his feet.

When looking up hot tears burned down
For his aching bones he did not care
Even through disgrace and hurt
He rejoiced to see his bag still there.

Scraping slowly along the path
That led him to a makeshift shed
He looked around at four hungry faces
Sleeping in a cardboard bed.

They heard him enter and awoke
Hopeful eyes asked questions old,
He held his treasure up to see
A wealth of riches- scores of gold.

All gathered round excitedly
As spilled the contents on the floor
leftovers of meals so sloppily nibbled,
But a feast for the starving hopeless poor.

Amongst whoops of the purest joy
Hoots of delight did fill the air,
As today they could eat all their hearts' desire
-What tomorrow would bring- they did not care

****

TO LIVE A WHOLE LIFE

To live a whole life
on a memory- it
can be done.

Reliving that instant
again and again
in a time warp,
remembering just how it was
when a chance meeting evoked
a flame of excitement that danced
inside, causing those butterflies
to waltz crazily within. Or when you
mixed up words
saying the opposite of
what you really meant to.
Making you curse yourself for
not saying all that filled your heart
and consumed your soul, for
appearing the infinite fool, tongue twisted
and incoherent. But did
you really need words to
convey the sparkle of your eyes whenever
you met? Why should you have had to
speak the obvious that everyone else readily noticed?

At that time everything revolved
around when you would next meet- and until
then, just reminiscing over
what had just been said or passed through closed
lips.
It was as sure as the early tide that sweeps in every
morning
from its romancing the twinkling
stars and moonlight on
mischievous waves the night before.
You thought that everything was so certain,
fated together, meant for each other –

How would you have known that self assurance
could prove so detrimental?
That an inner voice could sometimes
deceive and mislead, or that shared
laughter, treasured dreams and playful banter
essentially meant nothing to another?

But 'tis cruel and vindictive this world we are in
where the cunning and shrewd
get ahead, manipulating their paths
straight through the imaginings of
foolish dreamers.

So be it, malicious fate.

Because, to live a whole life
on a memory- it
can be done.

****

HISTORY IS WITNESS

History is witness
That man
Proved unworthy to inherit
The earth from its creator.
Since time immemorial
We fought,
But why?
For the land that would
Eventually house his grave,
Or the thrones that
Cursed sons against their fathers?

When given power,
We abused;
When opportunity arose
We plundered;
Have we all fallen
From the eyes of each other,
Or just ourselves?
Since oil is much thicker than water,
Tears hold no value
And blood is expendable.

Have we finally come full circle
To the barbarism of the dark ages?
Because now,
Everything is much easier.
Cry all you want;
Scream all you can;
No one will hear you
As justice is blind.
And hearts have crystalised
To the hardest of diamonds.
Cutting through the very core
of humanity itself.

****

TEARS ARE NOT A SIGN OF WEAKNESS

Tears are not a sign of weakness
For when the strongest of men cry, they
Show how vulnerable is the heart that
Never misses a beat.

Even when it is weighed
Down by the burdens of yesterdays, the untiring
Rhythm goes on. Pumping existence into tired veins
That know no other sustainer of life. How easy
It is for some to relieve reservoirs of emotions
While others can store up a dam
Of passion.

But overflow it will. Someday,
Sometime. The walls will have to give way to
That crushing force generating pressure
That gives way to a flood. Do not
Keep it all to yourself as you
May unleash the tsunami inside
That will endeavour to sweep
You away to nothingness.

****

MY MODEST BOUQUET

I saw my grandmother yesterday,
Looking graceful, radiant as always.
Her thoughtful gaze told me she knew
What I wanted to ask, her reassuring
Look, spoke volumes of the wisdom that graced her
Bright, ever-seeing eyes.

She smiled at my question, and held
My hand in that soft ,warm, clasp.
At once, I felt at peace and knew that
All would be well, and again
Was back in time, when young burning tears
Were always soothed in loving arms.

She always made me laugh when
innocently telling me secrets others had
whispered to her- winking mischievously
that I must tell no other. Or when she
insisted on watching the latest
horror films while nearly jumping out
of her chair and
screaming behind a hand held in front of her eyes.

I'll never forget her message. She gave it to me years
ago telling me she knew what path I should take.
I followed her guidance and am eternally grateful.

So, I sighed gently and
Looked at the flowers I had picked
Early morning, and laid my modest bouquet
On the soft earth.
I smiled down at her, feeling an
Enormous relief, knowing I would see her again
When I closed my eyes tonight.

****

WE NEED TO FIND

Pick a flower from
any garden you find. It
is up to you to separate
weeds from blooms. Sometimes
there will be acres galore, now
and again the fields
will be few.

In the harshest of
days, the wilderness may
shrivel and dry
-parched from a cruel summer
sun. As
seasons entwine, be sure to
be there when buds start to beautify and
fragrance the air.

Pick the roses from
thorns, don't be scared by their
sting, who are there to intimidate admirers,
but take these blooms
you must, to adorn
your own backyard where
the sun shines only
for you.

And then when ever
needed, you will have a wealth
of splendor from where,
when ever the need,
a bouquet of your choice
can be given to those
who need a garland of love.

****

NEVER BECOME A POET

Never become a poet because
It is really a test of endurance.
Not so much of your patience when trying
To sort out complex thoughts entangled
Inside your head, but for family and friends
Who inwardly cringe when you approach
Them paper in hand.

So what if your heart is awash with the
Miseries of the world- do you really think words
Can make a difference? But oh,
For that confounded vanity
Always getting the better of you; it keeps
One putting pen to paper.
Eccentric, fanatic, single minded
That's what all think, and while they converse
Readily enough, the slightest inclination of your
Narrating something recently composed will
Drive all but a very
Selected few away from your midst.
-better to keep quiet and remain popular.

Why bother with the marvels of the world
And why the fragility of a single snowflake
Enchants you, as it may unleash such an immense power
When tiny crystals come together. Or why
The morning dew that has been sent to
Cleanse early blooming buds, seem like
Drops of crystalline diamonds- a message from
The night sent to further adorn
Nature's beauty.
Are you so vain to think others can't see
This exquisiteness too?

Spare a thought for those dear
To you, and what they feel when
At a much anticipated gathering
You get that sudden
Urge to recite a latest work- as
Your family scan the floor in dismay.

So remember, never become a poet
Or your world will never be the same.

****

JUST A LITTLE CARE

Little child
With no shoes,
Don't waste your tears of pearls-
Because nobody cares.

Old woman
Who lost sons to war,
Sob not for loved ones gone-
As nobody cares.

Broken soul,
With no strength left,
Think not for humanity lost-
And why nobody cares.

Powerful man
Who stands towering tall,
Sleep soundly every night-
As you need not care.

****

THOSE VICIOUS OF TONGUE

Those vicious of tongue
With scalding words
Leave others to lick their wounds
When they have been near.
As jealousy and lies harden the heart
And blacken the soul,
It makes it a heavy burden
To bear and carry around.

Unlike those who step lightly,
Being the sweetest of language
And cheerful of spirit.
Trailing paths of joy
When conversing with others.
Offering soft words of comfort
To many an injured heart.
They have no worries
In wearing their consciousness
Which is as light and weightless as a feather.

****

SPRING

Spring, spring, is everywhere,
You can feel it in the air
Birds are singing all day long
Now the winter clouds have gone.

Roses red are in full bloom
Nightingales sing out their tune
As the buds turn into flowers
We rejoice in natures powers.

Towering trees fan out their leaves
Which flutter in the mellow breeze
A happy feeling's in the air
Now that spring is everywhere.

****

A LAND OF BEAUTY

A land of beauty-
Nature's dream,
A valley where the rivers gleam.
Amongst the peaceful, scenic view
There lurks a terror which is true.
The agonies of tortured souls,
Their silent screams that are ignored.
When will the world start to hear
The suffering cries that pierce Kashmir.

****

ENJOYING BASANT !

It's true; the world's a house of sorrow,
Who knows the outcome of tomorrow?
With all the 'crores' we had to borrow,
Bad memory is bliss!

Unemployment's on the rise,
Frustration, then, is no surprise,
Health and wealth stay on our minds,
Reality is grim.

So, don't you think our nation needs,
A time to let all tensions ease,
Enjoying in the spring time breeze,
The festival Basant!

****

TRUE LOVE

When she took a look at you
It was love at first sight,
She was enchanted by your smile
-your eyes shining bright.

She put in you her trust
By filling up an empty life
She wanted to be more
Than just her husband's wife.

We told her you would leave
That you really would n't stay
She said that separation,
Was a long way away

Every breath she now takes
Whispers your name
Try as she might
Now her life is not the same.

Her memories live on
Fresh like the morning dew,
So go, her only child,
To pastures new.

****

SILENT TEARS

You are you, and I am me,
And that's the way it's meant to be.

Our journey's roads, diverse and far,
Have turning paths that seem bizarre.
I live my life - As you do yours,
I know not how each soul endures,
The cruelty this world provides
Creating starving, suffering lives.

As long as I am safe and sound
I will not hear the grief profound,
That fills your heart and blows your mind
-The anguished souls of all mankind.
The streams of tears that now run dry
Those eyes which ask the question- 'Why?'

As long as I have comfort near
It will be hard for me to hear,
The silent begging for relief
To reinstate that lost belief,
That man was born an equal being
One and the same- with equal feeling.

But-you are you, and I am me
Is that the way it's meant to be?

****

CLIMB ANY MOUNTAIN

For every mountain big or small
Every building short or tall
Any fence or highest wall,
Those who climb will sometimes fall.

Its bouncing back that's hard to do
To smile again when feeling blue,
But to ourselves we must be true
To find the strength we never knew.

Don't ever think 'it can't be done'
In fact these words apply to none,
Keep up the fight you have n't won
Acquire the powers of the rising sun.

Appreciate the things you do
Don't name your talents as just a few
Look beyond what's hard for you
Keep your triumphs in your view.

Relationships will come and go,
Like little seeds they start to grow
Amid this all be sure to know
Who's a friend and who's a foe.

Although we struggle most the while
It's little things that make you smile
You may run a yard or walk a mile
Its getting there that is worthwhile.

Along this stumbling, rambling, race
With all the obstacles we face
Your loved ones need a special place,
Give them in your heart the biggest space.

And when life's voyage draws to its end
We look back at time that we did spend
There should be no broken hearts to mend
As we have been our own best friend.

****